Black Girl Shattered

Black Girl Shattered

Sheri Purpose Hall

39 WEST
PRESS

39 WEST PRESS
Kansas City, MO
www.39WestPress.com

39 WEST
P R E S S

First Edition: February 2017

ISBN: 978-1-946358-01-1

Library of Congress Control Number: 2016958895

This book is a work of fiction. Names, characters, places, dates, and incidents are products of the author's imagination, or are used fictitiously, satirically, or as parody. Any resemblance to actual persons, living or dead, business establishments, events, or locales is entirely coincidental.

10 9 8 7 6 5 4 3 2 1

Design, Layout, Edits: Jeanette Powers & j.d.tulloch

For all of the
Heartbroken
Identity-fractured
Life-shattered black girls everywhere ...

For everyone who watched them crumble
And possibly crumbled along with them ...

For every
Remedy
Magical healer
Waymaker ...

For all of those who
Make ...

This book is for you.
This book is for us.
All.

Contents

Sand

Clay

Broken Shards

Faux Repair

Gold Repair

Foreword

Sheri Purpose Hall is many things. She is a kind and gentle spirit who brings a sense of warmth and tenderness to every room she enters. She is a gale force wind who wrecks microphones and blows back the head of anyone who happens to be in the audience when she takes the stage. She is a peacemaker and an activist, a preacher and healer, a mother and a mentor. To borrow the words of Walt Whitman, she contains "multitudes." She effortlessly weaves her spirituality, black consciousness, and femininity into a tapestry of words that have often left me breathlessly in awe. I cannot count the times that I have heard her read a poem and thought to myself, "Daayuuum! I wish I had written that." Over the years, Sheri and I have had several opportunities to perform together or to work with one another on various projects, and in the process, I have become one of her biggest fans.

The volume of poems you now hold in your hands is further evidence of the Black Girl Magic we have come to marvel at over the past year. Sheri has gifted us with a special collection that, like her, is many things: part memoir, part feminist manifesto, part sacred text, part Black Studies thesis, and fully poetic. This book will surely minister to you in a way that few literary works are able to achieve. Take for instance the poem "Mary," which is at once an homage to the mother of the Christ child but also a cry for help for all the other Marys who have been horribly forsaken by a culture that continues to devalue femininity:

> *Where is Mary?*
> *Somewhere being trafficked*
> *Being molested by Uncle Ricky*
> *The fam' think he cool*
> *'Cause he got that sticky*
> *Puttin' books before boys*
> *Puttin' career before peers for so long*
> *The time for her to make a family*
> *Has come and gone*

Or witness the stunning vision she creates in "August 11, 2016: Re-imagined," in which her head of hair becomes Medusa-like and exacts vengeance upon the blinded-by-privilege white woman who dared to touch it:

> *She attacked **MY CROWN!***
> *Immediately*
> *The blue hair bush*
> *Erupted into venomous snakes*
> *Wrapped the white rope arms*
> *Strangled them*
> *Cutting off the circulation to her tentacles*

Yes, this astounding volume of verses makes it abundantly clear that Sheri Hall is fulfilling her *purpose* in glorifying God and edifying us mere mortals with the awesome power of her words.

— Glenn North

Introduction

My grandmother could knit, crochet, sew, sow, reap, rip, prepare, cook, and mend—anything, anytime, anywhere. This was her lifelong profession. She was a feisty quick wit with a swift backhand and could whip with a switch as if she were the wind and the switch was still attached to the tree. She was privately loud but publicly reserved, loving yet harsh, and full of trouser wearing gumption; yet she did all of her gardening in a jean skirt and flesh-toned knee highs. She was all things ladylike and fire.

I remind my mother of her.

For a living, both of my grandparents worked for the school district. Education and information was very important to them and they made sure that all six of their children could speak properly, read fluently, and type proficiently. My grandmother was a secretary at a school, grandfather was a custodian. He was very different from my grandmother, almost the opposite some would say. His serene demeanor countered her spunk and gave a strange balance. His voice was calm and gentle like a cleansing breeze that softly sweeps away all faults and reveals hidden treasure. His mannerisms were the same, calm, quiet, cool. However, he was no pushover. He had a shotgun; tucked it away in the house with bullets at the ready.

He was an able warrior and protector, disguised as subdued.

I suppose my mother got sewing and working in the school district from both of her parents. Outside of my grandparents, my mother had a close family friend/play mother who was a seamstress. We had occasion to spend hours at her house, helping her to prepare for weddings, where she would sew, create, and dress entire wedding parties. In that house, I have seen whole lives and families come together from simple scrap material and tacky glue. Although I always saw the joy in families coming together, I still returned home as a single child to a single mother. Somehow, I know this affected her too.

My mother hid her soft.
I suppose that's what you do when you do it all.

I'm sure it was predictable, that I would also enjoy working with my hands. I am a crafter, the kind of woman who uses a glue gun for everything from décor to functionality. I keep many broken things because I know that somehow I will be able to make that broken, used, ripped, torn thing useful again. I learned this out of necessity and habit. I come from a long line of people who, when only starting with dirt and scraps, are able to envision the end of full scale projects, life changes, and solid families. I come from a long line of people who relied on the work of their own hands to get it done.

I come from a long line of mixed-tender and hard.

I stumbled upon an art form I knew nothing about: Kintsugi. As a crafter and a keeper of broken things, I naturally wanted to try it out. With the innocent, excited eyes of a preschooler, I began my research. I found myself, my story, and the story of my people within the methods and pieces of art of another culture.

This Japanese art, of adding precious metals and rare tree lacquers to what was once seemingly trash, gripped me. The process takes time, patience, experience, and costly materials; it was a huge investment into broken things. When the gold repair is finished, the new piece is strong, waterproof, exquisite, and more valuable than the original unbroken piece. And more importantly, the piece is useful again. Kintsugi calls for the cracks to become a part of the design, illuminating, revealing, and celebrating the history instead of suppressing it. It was both symbolic and beautiful.

Women are the same.

The Kintsugi pieces spoke to me. It was as if the pieces had lives and souls and names. They were all women. They were all from God. The potter molded us with curves, made us vibrant, shiny, and useful. We were fired in a kiln, baked under immense pressure, and when we emerged, we were a thing of beauty, polished and ready for service. Then, it happened: a hurt here, a fall there, a whoops here, and an on-purpose there. We found ourselves chipped, scratched, broken, beaten, and weathered.

Black women are this.

Through this art, I saw the black experience as told through the hands of Japanese people. I'm sure that their experiences both in America and Japan can be seen in this art. But for some reason, while viewing it, I could see was myself. I could see black women and how we continue to reinvent ourselves. We mend ourselves, finding that our brokenness is not a thing to be ashamed of but something that adds character and beauty. We are talented and dynamic. We are not meant for shelf-sitting and dust-collecting. In our day-to-day existence, we are meant to bring glory. We are imperfect vessels, perfected and beautified by all that we have endured throughout time. Our histories, oral traditions, tragedies, and triumphs were not meant to loiter on the underside of rugs. Our experiences are gold, and they make us stronger. The showcasing of this gold reminds the admirer that heroes exist, that healing is possible, and that survival is necessary.

We make art out of damage.

Surviving and moving forward from old wounds is hard, especially when each day so many new traumas are being heftily dumped into our psyches. This notion makes me reflect on my grandparents. Their lives were not always easy; they weren't far removed from slavery. People they knew, grew up with, and could touch had been either slaves or sharecroppers. In fact, they did some sharecropping themselves. They lived through the Great Depression, World Wars I and II, the Civil Rights Movements, free love, and the Cold War. My grandmother saw the Berlin Wall go up and lived to see it come down. They lived and watched as this world changed, as tragedies and triumphs kept happening. By the end of their lives, their memory banks must have looked like a stockpile of authenticated periodicals, monuments, and pictures.

But as they aged, the evidence of dementia grew in both of them. It wasn't all that noticeable in grandma, but in grandpa, it was pronounced and eventually transitioned into Alzheimer's. There came a time when she was no longer able to care for him, and it became necessary to place him in a home where he could receive from nurses and doctors the kind of 24 hour care that he required. After he passed away, grandmother's Alzheimer's quickly set in.

Sometimes we need to forget.

While visiting and caring for my grandparents, they told me stories of a different time. To them, I was never Sheri. I was one of their children. As their memories waned, I wasn't offended at being forgotten for them. I was flattered that they thought I was my mother or one of my aunties. My grandmother gleefully recalled her time at school and at conventions, describing in detail all the different nationalities of beautiful people she had met. She appreciated people from all over the world and the natural art found in soft chins, round cheeks, and brown skin.

My grandfather, on the other hand, was a bit different. The nursing home was mandated to keep his hat from him. If his hat went onto his head, then he was surely about to walk out of the door. That was the equation: HAT+HEAD=DOOR. One time, he got a hold to his hat and left the nursing home, making his way on foot to 2519 College Avenue. In his mind, he was leaving his job at Lincoln and heading home to his wife.

Sometimes we need to remember.

Please journey with me through these poems, epistles, and essays. Remember our stories. Find the brokenness. Find the gold. Hold it close.

— Sheri Purpose Hall

Sand

I can either refine, be refined, or harm.

Dear Life

Dear Life,

I think I am supposed to be gritty like sand in order to survive you.

I think I am supposed to be the kind of thing that can smooth edges yet be put through the fire and made into something transparent and easily broken.

I think I am supposed to be the type of thing that when easily broken has the ability to cut and draw blood.

Yet you seem to want me to possess sand while being timeless—like a faulty hour glass spilling its contents, spreading itself way too thin across an unforgiving restless sea.

Somehow you want me to stick around and just sink in, be unseen and unheard but functional.

Maybe I am full of myself.

At any rate, it doesn't change what you require. And your requirements don't change my composition.

I can only be who I am.

I can either refine, be refined, or harm.

Choose who you want me to be.

Signed,

Every Woman

P.S. Choose wisely.

No.

I AM
Capable
Proficient
Potent
Skilled

I CAN DO
Mine
Yours
This
That

I AM NOT ALL
Comprehensive
Heap
Bulk
Mass

I WILL NOT BE EVERYTHING
Anymore
For anyone
There are limits
And I AM enough

No. #2

His *"No."*
Is an obelisk,
Tall and free standing
In the open space for the world to see.

Her *"No."*
Is bound by a straight jacket
And thrown into a padded room,
Closed in and locked.

His *"No."*
Is hard stone:
Accepted.

Her *"No."*
Must wear white:
MUST wear white to be respected.

No. #3

Why must my "No." be padded for you?
Is it to sustain your belief that women are complicated?
Is a hard "No." too simple a sentiment?

No.
Capital *N*, lowercase *o*, **PERIOD**.
No, with no explanation.
No boyfriend, husband, dad, or other man to pad it.
No explanation of belief system and background.
No explanation of relationship and sexual past.
No explanations.
No entertaining a conversation.
No accepting the offer.
No it's not flattering.
No and no thank yous to give.
No.
The word is **No**.
No.
Don't.
Dead not delayed, done.
Firm, final, finished.
Not, null, negatory, nix, nah.
Shut down, shut up, soldered, sealed, sailed, sunk.
Non-compliant.
Non-agreeing.
Non-consenting.
Non-acceptance.
No.
That's it.
That's all.
No.
My "**No**." is enough.

Mary

•

Mary—

Teenage virgin valuable beyond rubies
Woman of color and virtue carrying the salvation of man
Pedestaled and worshiped by Catholicism
Her descendants degraded and buried

Who protects Mary?

Fell prey to bullet spray at 7-11
Fell prey to bullet spray in her living room
Body found at the bay
News filled with pictures of all the little Marys gone too soon

3-year-old little girl on Chestnut
Shot in the stomach
Raped in broad daylight on 43rd Street
Nobody said nuthin', like they ain't seen nuthin'

300 Marys simply carried away
Never to be seen again
The remembrance of their existence
Chalked up to a quickly dissipating hashtag: *BringBackOurGirls*

Where is Mary?

Somewhere being trafficked
Being molested by Uncle Ricky
The fam' think he cool
'Cause he got that sticky

Puttin' books before boys
Puttin' career before peers for so long
The time for her to make a family
Has come and gone

They talk 'bout Mary 'cause she looks too European
They talk 'bout Mary 'cause she looks too African
Pit Mary against Mary with team light- team dark-skin
Thick, shapely or slim, there's no honor for any shape she's in

She's in the school bathroom being 2 boys train of *thot*
Dad didn't teach her the proper train of thought
Thought those boys liked her 'cause she thought she liked them
'Cause melanated entertainment trained her thoughts

Thought the only way to be celebrated on every hook they play
(By the likes of Nate Dog and T-Pain) was to get down this way
Thought she would marry a Hosea
If she'd shed virtue and become a lil' more Gomer

Watched her sons killed over and over for nothing and everything
Martyred and murdered as she was at His feet
Don't you dare ask why she weeps
Don't you dare ask why she buggin' or why she strugglin'

Where is Mary?

Started taking drugs today
Is contemplating suicide
Ain't been herself for so long
Forgot she was divine

Mary, why are you dying?

Trying so hard to see the angels
Forgot the angels were coming to speak to you
Blessed art thou among women
Blessed is the fruit of thy womb

Did you forget that God was supposed to come through?
You are the canal of virtue
Birthing miracles, businesses, ministries, communities
Lifelong connections that save lives

Why you so independent?
You were to be protected
Your son left someone to look after you
You ain't gotta be out here alone

I need you
I love you
You have to love you
You have to love each other

We all we got
They *tryna* take us out and we goin' gently
This ain't that goodnight
Please, you gotta fight

Mary, where are you?

My Shadow and Me

To all the people who ever told a woman not to get "beside herself."

Beside myself
May be the only ally I see
May be the only person on my side
May be the only person
Who
Catches my side eye just right
Knows when it's time to fight
Knows what my fear looks like
Understands my voice
Encourages it to be heard
Stands beside me
Stans beside me
Supports me like no other has before
May be the only one who loves me to the core
Loves me honestly, requiring no reward

MishMash

I am a mixture
A mess of proper grammar and vernacular
A patchwork of complex mathematics and Ebonics
A collection of Queen's English and American Standards

I am an operatic mixtape
Corner beat box concerto

I am liquid
With a messy habit
Of running over
Of disrespecting containment

I am limitless
Encompassing greatness

In short
I am extremely dope

Mystique

She is the consistent question mark at the end of your sentence,
Sentencing you to search for all her answers.

She is the opera void of her plight
But full of her divas.

She is the teacher molding *Dangerous Minds,*
Blindsided by poverty (non-existent in the movie).

She is midnight confessions of love
And daytime absences.

She is Pornhub lust
And public disgust.

Her skin is flickering onyx sparkle.
Her stomach is a pillow-like waiting place.

Her thighs are abundant and round,
Protecting tanzanite mysteries.

She is a winding hipped conductor
With Nature playing to her metronome.

She is what you want
But are afraid to admit.

She is responsibilities
Heaping shoulder blades,

Sitting in mounds,
Rolling down sides,

Settling into fat,
Sinking between vertebrae,

Crowning and overflowing her small,
Traveling to see the glory of her split,

Getting stuck in the top crevasse,
And standing tall through the pain of all this.

She is the woman of your dreams,
A day-walking magical mistress.

She is a phenomenal, mystical conundrum,
And her charms break all your boundaries.

Whip My Hair (Full Version)

I whip
my hair with or without weave.
I whip when it is flowing and cascading:
silky or yaky, relaxed straight, loc'd up, round 'fro, and nappy.

I whip
when my hair is long,
in a bun, in an updo,
or in a ponytail.

I whip
when my hair has too much gel
or is stiff from spritz,
even when I go on strike and ain't combing it.

I whip
with and without makeup;
arch or no arch in the eyebrow,
my face still has the same expressiveness.

I whip
no matter how I'm dressed:
wrinkled, fresh pressed,
in workout gear, business attire, or a formal dress.

I whip
my hair when you can't see it's whipping,
while it's in a head wrap,
in a bonnet, in curlers, or pinned down.

I whip
when my hair is short,
slicked down, faded down,
taper bob'd, or twisted.

I whip
my neck in the attitude and tradition of my ancestors;
my earrings dangle dangerously,
like darts shimmering and swinging.

I whip
with *dagger-like* confidence,
derailing every derogatory description
of my tresses, of my beauty, of my people, of my *me*.

I whip
my hair in the traditions of the Divine Nine, Flo Jo,
Dorothy Dandridge, Harriet Tubman, freedom, fame, fortune,
firsts, and like your granny, I'll whip you.

I whip
my hair because I am beautiful and didn't always think I was,
because I am joyfully defiant,
because I am different and proud of it.

I whip
reckless and willingly because I'm feelin' myself,
flashing a side smile, eyelashes fluttering,
hand on hip, celebrating all of me.

I whip
because I create the windfalls of revolution
with one twist of my neck, one look of my eye:
a non-verbal communication that can bring a community to rise.

I whip
because it is mine:
mine to flaunt,
mine to exercise.

I whip
because I am THAT chick,
and who I am
deserves some shine.

August 11, 2016: Reality

It was fruits of labor
Come to harvest
Air strawberry sweet
Sticky as sugar blood
Oozing from over ripened berries

Humid August from mild winter
A Kansas City tradition
Instant skin melt
Outside of air condition

I was blue
A Kansas City tradition
Royals game day blue shirt
And contrasting black shorts
Royals game day blue
And black **contrasting**
Fluffy, nappy, curly hair

She
A middle-aged white woman
Short cut brunette
Slippery curly hair
Entered the door
Quickly approached
Fondly smiled
Suggesting **childhood memories**

The light in her eyes
Flickered and danced
Like the *BFF* **I forgot existed**

And I
Awkward in my embarrassment
Smiled back

Feeling inadequate
Desperately trying to recapture her
Face in my mindscape

She gave the loooong
Hiiiiii!
Then said
Well ain't you caaauuuteee!

As she greeted
It seemed there was a magnetic pull
A force that instantaneously drew
Her whole hands to my head

In that instant I immediately felt deceived
My embarrassment amplified to anger and agony

Frisked like a dog in public
Like she saw me through the window
Like she had to pet Fido
(It ain't like white folks name their dogs King and Queen)

Was she here to buy me?

Fists clenched
   Still smiling

Blood pressure raised
   Still smiling

Tears welling
   Still smiling

Heart racing
   Still smiling.

Does anyone here see that I have been **violated**?

ANYONE IN THE WHOLE STORE?
HELP!!!!

HER HANDS ARE ON MY PERSON!
HELP!!!!

THIS SMILE IS A CHARADE!
HELP!!!!

That 60 seconds of century was too long
And instead of painting her black and blue
My **impotent fists** still clenched
Failed to respond

And when she walked away
I walked outside to the van
Maintaining the **undistraught**
Demeanor

Upon entering the van
I was greeted by an audience of my children
They asked
"Mom, who was that?"

August 11, 2016: Re-Imagined

I was blue
A Kansas City tradition
Royals game day blue shirt
And contrasting black shorts
Royals game day blue
And black contrasting
Fluffy, nappy, curly hair

She
A middle-aged white woman
Short cut brunette
Slippery curly hair
Entered quickly
Approached fondly
Smiled
Suggesting childhood memories

The light in her eyes
Flickered and danced
Like the *BFF* I forgot existed

And I
Awkward in my embarrassment
Smiled back
Feeling inadequate
Desperately trying to recapture her
Face in my mindscape

Little did I know
She was a menace

Her long-lost *BFF* disguise disabled
My normal defensive mechanisms
Activating displaced embarrassment

Then IT happened!
SWOOOSH!!!

Her arms transformed into long white ropes
Wrapped around my head
Mummifying my hair

Her tentacle like phalanges
Dug through the blue bush camouflage
Slithered across my scalp
As if to uproot my braided armor

She attacked **MY CROWN!**

Immediately
The blue hair bush
Erupted into venomous snakes
Wrapped the white rope arms
Strangled them
Cutting off the circulation to her tentacles

Noooooooooo! she yelled

I had her locked in my grip
Then suddenly her head split
Gobs of black smoke bellowed
And the once menacing figure went limp

The smoke took multiple forms
All with noodle arms

As their shapes solidified
They turned to pasty colored blobs
Oozing with personal space
Penetrating wonderment
Glistening eyes and wide smiles
All repeating in unison
"I love your hair"

The snakes loosened the grip
On the listless carcass
And as it dropped to the ground
It created a dust cloud

With super suction
I inhaled the dust from the air
Then blasted the legionnaires

They fell on impact
But bounced off the floor
And with each bounce
There came more
Till their number was 5004!

At that moment
I knew what I had to do
I am a blue haired black girl
One of the most mystical beings in existence.

I had to use … **THE MAGIC!**

As my arms opened
Electricity built
Surged between my fingers
Creating a ball of crackling light

Bigger and bigger the light grew

Then ... **CLAP!**

The ball burst into the sky
Rained droplets of common sense onto my enemies
Singed their investigatory instincts
Causing the once reaching noodles to retreat

The blast caused me to whirl and spin
Ascending into the air

Beams of violatory-disrespectarocious eradicators
Shot from my fingernails
Blasting and annihilating the white blobs

As they melted into puddles of weeping privilege
The cries of "I wanted to see what it felt like"
And "I just wanted to touch it"
Decreased from shrill to nil
Till nothing was left but the residue of white tears

The friendly, intrusive, petting zoo monster was obliterated

And as the smoke cleared
I returned to my normal soft, sweet, melanated, majestic form
Straightened my blue crown and looked around to see
The horror of the other inactive, less brave, petting zoo monsters

They were shocked!
Mortified!
TERRIFIED!

All moved backwards with their hands clasped behind their backs

YES!
THIS DAY
They learned
(Though it may be alluring and gorgeous in all its glory)
NEVER violate the space of another human without consent

And

NEVER INVADE A BLACK WOMAN'S HAIR

The Funeral List

Dear Lord **n' WHOEVA ELSE** listenin'

Ya'll gon' hafta control yo chi'ren an' kin folk 'round my casket! I will be respected in my death. Do you hear? Respected! And I know, **LAWD I KNOW,** my righteousness is but filthy rags to you, but still ...

1. Tell them old lonely women and fast-tailed young ones to wear clothes, please ... and not size 2T! **Grown woman clothes that cova' evrathang!** I have never seen mo' thigh than I have eva seen at a funeral. Skirts so high I began to think all the knees were **LOWERED.** Wearin' a shirt lookin' like the cleavage goes to the navel. Got theyself all perked and propped up like corner warmers. It's 3 degrees and these women look like it's 70. **It's an OUTRAGE!** You are most certainly not going to come to my funeral and run off with any man from my family. No no! The men in my family respect themselves and **would not be caught dead with anything like you**.

In Public.

But LORD,

2. Just in case any of the men are lookin' (and I know there will be some), **LORD STRIKE 'EM DOWN, LORD!** Salivatin' o'er women in the church house, sweatin' like it's hot, grinnin' and such! **Control yo self!**

3. **Preach the gospel!** 'Specially for the hearing of the heathens mentioned in numbers 1 and 2.

4. Please keep all comments to less than 2 minutes and have someone assigned to **turn off the mic at 1 minute and 59 seconds.** Any longer than that, they makin' stuff up or tellin' stuff they ain't 'sposed to! **Either way, shut it ALL THE WAY down!**

a. Goin' along with the subject of the **long-winded people,** please make sure that there are **mints** located at the **front door,** with the **ushers,** with all **family members,** beside the **tissues** and the **sign in book.** It's bad enough that people want to publicly blubber but to have some **stankin' blubberin'** is another issue entirely and should be avoided **at ALL COSTS.**

5. *Can you* **make sure the funeral singer CAN sing,** knows my name, and knows the lyrics to the songs? '**Nuff said.** Oh, don't look at me. I have SEEN IT! Folk at the funeral murdering the person's name as they lay in the casket saying, "Sis. K K Ka... Ron?" **IT'S SIS KAREN, DUMMY. GET IT RIGHT!** It ain't like I got one of these chopped to bits capitals in the middle, hyphenated, apostrophe, accent-marked, ill-spelled mess of a name, names. Is that **TOO** much to ask?

6. Please, **Please, PLEASE** don't let these people put my picture on a t-shirt that these raggedy folks gonna wear once, neglecting to iron!!! They do this in the most **embarrassing** colors. I don't want my face on a hot pink, plaid, neon yellow, electric blue, hunter green army fatigue background or any other embarrassment. You do everything but behave like a child of God. Then, that shirt with my face on it gets ripped off of a funky body, only to be balled up in the corner of a dirty room smelling like old socks **and melting the eyebrows off my picture!**

Yes Lord! Which takes me to ...

7. Regarding my makeup: **PLEASE DRAW MY EYEBROWS ON RIGHT!** And for the love of ALL that is Holy, **Don't "black face" me or paint me ASHY!** Is it too much to ask for the right color foundation? I am so sure I will already have some in my kit at home. **USE IT!**

8. **Any and all forms of screaming and falling out are prohibited.** The meanest ushers, please stand **ON GUARD** at the front of the room! And they have my personal permission

to **KNOCK** the first person to start hollerin' who ain't under the spirit of the Holy Ghost!

9. I want a *repass* with class. **Turn no one away.** I have friends that were closer than family. I want everyone to come, laugh, and eat. Open the doors and play the music like I have opened my heart to all. **After all, they survived life with me,** and I am hard. I can't begrudge the people a little chicken. **It's the least I can do.**

And finally ...

10. When we rise with the pallbearers lifting me up, escorting me out those doors, the people betta stand and clap with a roar of joy (and laughter) for a life well lived. **All the crying should have been done when you found out I died.** I go to a far better place, and you get my funeral: a day of celebration. **I know my life. It is beautiful and full. And at the time of my death, it will have bloomed and run its course.** It will be celebrated as such, because I know where I'm goin'. **And after a life of hard work, it is never a sad occasion to return home.**

Signed,

Honestly & Peacefully At Rest

Conquering Death in the Wake of Tragedy for a Soul That is Finally Free

Hello Death
   We welcome pain
      Greet you
         Overcome
            We celebrate
               We rest in spirit
                  Eulogizing
                     Home going life
            Slain
                     Life going home
                  Eulogizing
              Spirit in rest
            We celebrate
         We overcome you
      Greet pain
   Welcome death
Hello

Clay

Boys will be boys ...
Until we teach them to be men.

Pavlov: To My Friend the Mistress

Let me get this straight ...

You called **HIM** a dog?

Not saying that he ain't grimy and wrong, but you chose to be on all fours in your boudoir. And though you saw a ring on his finger, you didn't see committed; you saw ready to commit ... saw this *brotha* in a moment of weakness and ran to go get it.

You called him a dog, after you chased his bone.

You had no complaints (flirtatious anticipation building), letting him know you were willing ... had no complaints with legs in the air.

There were no complaints when he was there ... no complaints when you were doing his laundry, washing dishes after dinners, snuggling under your sheets in the winter ... no complaints when sweat dripped off his nose onto your chin.

There were no complaints at his devilish midnight grin, drunk in lust to your delight. *Called you his star 'cause you only get shine at night.* And with the dimming light of morning, a brighter star set in.

The morning, when you got the warm rag to wipe the remnants of him from your leg ... when you looked in the mirror and told yourself you are worth more than this hit and miss: "Hits me up at night, and I am still a Miss instead of a Mrs."

The morning, when there was only one plate of eggs at your place but at his residence the eggs were eaten scrambled with toast.

He's kissing his children and his wife *with the same mouth that left you last night.*

And you, deeply saddened yet still hoping for your regularly scheduled lunchtime rendezvous: his mini vacation with you, escaping marital issues.

But this is real for you. No way for you to escape this lurking reality that you, mistress, are not the main Mrs. fulfilling your wishes through his kisses, only to be rudely awakened by him returning to this place he calls *"home."*

Whilst you have made every effort to comfort him, you still sleep alone most nights, unable to escape the thought that right now he is possibly having sex with his wife.

And in your mangled mental processes you believe this is wrong? Incorrect somehow? He makes his bed with you, yet he lays his head with who? Who is this chick, this other woman-wife-person? How dare she ... exist?

And you get pissed!

Blowing up his phone, making workplace appearances, taking your grievance to the Mrs., texting her his naked pictures.

Pretending to be some kind of friend, telling her all of your private business, talkin' out the side of yo' neck about him: "Girl, he a dog!"

You sho right, Pavlov.

And now that he has left you with nothing more than wet sheets and baby shoes, you want to come to the light and make things publicly right?!?!?

Girl, boooooooo!

But since disrespect has become common tool, I can see where you would think this is cool. Truth is, he would not have been able to dog you if you weren't the female dog he could run to.

Yet YOU called HIM a dog. You the one who set out on a mistress fantasy, opening yourself wider, hoping that he would fall in deep.

*You called HIM a dog because he went back **home**.*

The symbol of manhood in your life gone back to his wife, leaving you once again ...

Alone.

Pavlov: Torment

He caters to her, lovingly—texting sprees, wee morning hours talking—cultivating their relationship while I resort to Facebook stalking: snap shots of memories. Frequently, her smile a harsh reminder of how much he doesn't want me. Their relationship chronicled for my eyes to see.

He exercises brain and brawn, chest pumps for her to fawn ... prays to the Almighty ... praises the Almighty for this woman who can't possibly deserve him.

He cooks dinners, lunches, gives accolades and appreciation publicly.

What if he wanted me like I want him?

What if I stole his heart from her manicured hand?

I can see him and me posing for pictures, planning the future, enjoying the savor of romantic dinners.

He would be proud of me.

I want him more than she ... pursue him actively ... fix him lunches which he rejects ... perk up and poke out ... priss primp to put out.

And he walks past all this ~~ass~~ like it ain't even appealing! Like he ain't stared and meditated on the feeling! Like he ain't rested his head in this bust! Like he ain't had an occasion to slip into my sheets then pretend he kept **in**/fidelity.

He act like he don't see me! Make me feel unworthy! Oblivious to my self-improvements! Betterment meant to impress! Research to increase intelligence! Ignores advances! Refuses any engagement!

Diss-stanced short conversations and closed ended answers, yet I still chase, just for a taste.

He is my fantasy. The long time man of my dreams.

What if he loved me ... publicly? Made love to me ... passionately?

Holding me the way I know he holds her. Envisioning his lips and hands, the feeling of this man:

Gripping,
>   grabbing,
>>   pulling,
>>>   shivers.

>   Yet my bed ...
Antarctica, with no man to explore.

I have implored him to draw nigh, pulling him in with my mind and thighs. Yet he remains spirited away into the arms of this woman.

And I contemplate proceeding to proceedings, but ...

He is my husband!

And I just can't let him go that easily. **He used to love me**.

So I am stuck ... here, on the outside looking in,

Coveting what is rightfully mine.

Pavlov: Birth Defects

To comment or not to comment?

The question: a meme.

"Why do men cheat?"

The responses:

Because they can
Because we let them
Because they get away with it
Because they just do what they wanna do
Because they don't care about nobody else's feelings, UGH!

I mean, not to belittle their sentiments, but (ummm) no one asked why women cheat. And I'm sure if I were to ask why women carry on adulteress affairs with other women's men, some liberated, fist-pumping, *sista* girl would snap her neck and type, "Because she's a low down slut who needs to get her own."

Yes, I get it. Men still powerful.
Women still degraded.

It's like the worst and longest running *"yo mama"* joke ever, with children reduced to the bottom left quadrant of your *"single mother starter kit"* meme.

Asking "why men cheat" is about the same as asking why the trigger was pulled on a gun but not mourning the death of the murder victim. It is questioning a sexual relationship without acknowledging the product of the ejaculate: a whole new life brought into the world without acknowledgment.

I'm here,
and he don't claim me.

My birth certificate looks like a failed fill-in-the-blank test, transforming my mother into the plague, treating her as a disease and me a side piece side effect.

> *I am the itch that comes along with*
> *the illness you don't mention:*

> ### The unplanned addition.

> *I am proof that being fruitful*
> *can be problematic multiplication.*

I am the product of a cheating man and a mother who had been hurt by men so much her life that she was all right with only having him

> *sometimes,*
> *part-time,*
> *not really committed,*
> *being somewhat monogamous.*

She is an underserved population, spit on and talked about ... a person that the church doesn't even speak about (as if there were no Biblical examples of out of covenant babies).

> *But it's cool;*
> *Hagar also received God's blessing.*

> *Us Ishmaels go on to make great nations.*

Our existence drops bombs on wives with fragile hearts, calling illegitimate children and their mothers terrorists without accepting that the whole nation, laying in the bed beside them, orchestrated these incidents!

It's the perception of man and spouse as twin towers: all mighty and crumbling due to the evidence of some fly boning, crashing into your solid structures wrecking all!

Ground zeros come in all forms.
I visit crash sites other than mine all the time.

Most being called schools,
where we craft young minds
with eyes just like mine,
staring at me hopelessly
for a remedy of the pain
they have endured and seen.

And instead of a **remedy** or some form of **healing**, all you can offer is this raggedy meme.

Granny's Cultivation

Grandma had sweet potatoes in her garden

                        (Beautiful black boys

Not your regular tubers

                        (Smart, large minded restorers

Big brown boulders

                        (Children of promise

The kind that make you feel accomplished

                        (The kind that stand for something

The kind that add nutrients

                        (And stay close

Family loves it when they're at the table

                        (They embrace and are embraced

In all their glory

                        (Giving love to all, but especially Granny.

And Granny has a secret recipe, she butters them up

    (She gives them pure love, showing the young how it's done

Cinnamon, cloves, ginger, spices them up

                        (With truth, correction, and encouragement

Candies them syrupy sweet and fragrant

                        (Soothes them with her voice

Hums a sweet melody while preparing them for the fire

                        (Intercedes in prayer

Covers them to protect them from the heat

                        (Gives them time and space to think

And when they are done they are a delightful thing.

  (Making them ready for a family, and children, and the world.

Ready … to be consumed.

The Day My Son Takes Your Daughter on a Date: An Open Letter to Ya Girl's Moms Pops 'Nem

1. The fact that your daughter has agreed to go on a date with my son means that at some point she is open to penis. Yes, your child—beautiful and innocent—is a sexual being. She may still be a virgin, but she has made a conscious decision that she wants to try IT. Hopefully, PRAYERFULLY, she will wait until after she is married. I know you don't quite want to come to terms with this, but try IT she will. Deal.
   a. Dick
   b. Penis

2. If my son comes to your home and you (or her uncles, aunts, siblings, cousins, close family friends, acquaintances, hired hit men, or any otherwise unmentioned non-factors) flash steel in an attempt to intimidate him, know that he will turn and walk away. He will not puff out his chest in the attempt to seem macho for you; he will not cower to make you feel superior. Instead, he will proceed to his mode of transportation and call his parents. Then, we will come and **"talk"** with you about you feeling the necessity to threaten my child.

3. In the event that you do something *janky* like pray to God for homosexuality on your child, be aware that tho' you are strapped, she will be strapped too. Deal ... *doh.*
   a. She may become the womanizer you're scared of.
   b. Will you give her the same high-fives you give your son for multiple women?

4. Father of the girl my son chose to ask on a date, do not assume that he is the younger and or current version of you. You threatening harm upon him tells me more about who you are than who you think he is.

5. Mother of the girl my son chose to ask on a date, do not look at my son immediately imagining your daughter lonely and assume

he has the potential of disaster. You will not find a pillowy soft spot in my son to place all of your hardened dealings with men.

6. Let not your eyes gaze too long upon him with a steel cold stare. Let not your eyes attempt to make small what his parents have taught to stand strong. Your disdain hides behind your crooked smile, and in you, a spirit ready to pounce puts a fireball pit in his stomach. Don't cause him to flame you.

7. My son is a poet tree and won't be cut down without splintering a million pieces into your flesh.

8. My son is a King.
    a. Your child may be a peasant. The existence of lady parts and/or wealth does not deem her queen.

9. Father of the girl my son chose to ask on a date, before you pride yourself on raising a "heartbreaker," please remember the ONE who hurt you. At first, those women with electric thighs and shocking mouths that sent surges through your body were exciting, till you found yourself used, singed, void of energy, and motionless. Did you turn your daughter into the type of woman that broke you?
    a. She *bet* not break him. She *bet* not try to dice roll his heart on the ground because you taught her love was a game.
    b. We don't play those types of games: the kind that leave deep scars, the type that his wife will still clean and bandage when they are old.

10. Your daughter is growing. She is not your little princess anymore. Let go.

Signed,

A former little princess who bumped her head and still lived to tell the story.

P.S. Sometimes, it *was* me. They all weren't THAT bad.

Counterfeit O.G.

I

Showing the first hints of grey
Skin still smooth
Voice deep
Starting to have issues at the knees
Ain't no spring chicken
He's an end of summer persistent heat
But he think he a cold piece
Roars like a beast
Nomad back and forth
Searching for those on whom he may feast

Living like it's still his spring
Fresh dew
And chilly mornings
Perfect 70 degree days
And time to play
All while advising the other men
To put the toys away

II

They concrete all the softness out of their faces
When they see him
Tear ducts on restraint
Tightened throat struggles
To hide his secrets
Their embarrassment
No emotions emitted
No admittance to things whispered in ears
Done behind closed doors

Taking liberties from ladies
Copper beauties with flames in their hands
Eyes and mouths
They are statuettes collected for his trophy case

Things to be won
Conquered
Tamed
Because he is the only one that can do them right
Ain't nobody done them right unless it was him

They wouldn't dare out loud about him
Wouldn't dare bust him out
For bustin' 'em up
Bustin' self-images
Bustin' 'em to the core
Bustin' in 'em
Believing a good bustin'
Was all they really needed to act right
Is bustin' ever really wanted?
Requested?
Pleasurable?
I suppose it is when you're a buster.

III
They see him and constellations
Spring from their faces
Struck with doe-eyed admiration
Seeking his approval
Crumbling at anything less
Reminiscing on his heyday
On his chastisement
On his molding of them
He, a leader of men
A man's man
A disregarder of women
A manipulator of image
Public promenade and respect

They speak of him
And their chests puff out
Shoulders square
They posture themselves

As mere mortals speaking of the king
Womanizers walking in his footsteps
Privately and publicly
Carrying on his legacy

IV
He lived past 25
Irresponsibly

He lived past 25
With no stability

He lived past 25
Dropping seeds
On concrete wondering why nothing has grown

He lived past 25
And now receives
All the admiration and respect of a grandfather

He lived past 25
Recklessly
And now shows the *youngins* how it's done

He lived past 25
And due to this credential
Listens to no one

Blue in the Face or Deceased

You think of us fondly
Delicious peach nectar memories
All champagne bubbly
And intoxicating.
Maybe we were drunk.

The room was always tilted.
Somehow you were always
Effortlessly on the upside,
Sure footed
With nary a slip to be seen.

Then there was me.
Sliding down,
Skin rubbed raw,
Burning,
Crashing into a piss-filled corner,
Glass piercing,
Stabbing,
Slashing,
Deconstructing my solid figure to minced meat,
Head hitting the wall repeatedly.
Concussions.

Maybe that explains why I continued.
Maybe I didn't remember the hurt.
Maybe the room was so tilted
That I wasn't able to climb up.
Maybe I was drunk.

Maybe it wasn't your fault,
What happened to me
Every time we were together.
Maybe it was just that the room was tilted,
And I was drunk.

Yeah that's it!
The room,
The UNIVERSE,
Even the stars misaligned!
Or was that just *blurry* vision?

All of it was just wrong.
It kept me down
And you kept up,
Unscathed,
Pristine and holy.

Maybe I will write *that* poem.
Maybe you deserve *that* poem,
Not the sober one but the one still *inebriated*.

Just wait, hold on ...

Hold your breath ...

Hold ... *like you held on to me.*

Hold ... *like you held my joy.*

Hold ... *like you held my peace.*

Hold ... *like you hold my sleep, swapping dreams with night terrors.*

Hold ...

Never give up.

Trials of an Unclaimed Child: Love Me or Leave Me Alone

I have learned
more from your absence
than I ever would have learned
from your half-presence.

Thank you.

Trials of an Unclaimed Child:
Daddy Answer

Daddy did you remember to pray for me?
Did you think of me?
Did you find a place in your heart for me?
Did you?

I would like to say that I am beyond wondering
Why you weren't there?
Why you didn't care to claim me?
Took no part in naming me
But your makings are all over me

Took no part in raising me
Yet I inherited your genetic disease
Asthma arthritis allergies
Belly round diabetic possibilities
I look more like your side than I care to see
Yet you still managed to deny me

I would love to say that I forgave it all
And didn't write them Daddy hate poems
Wish I could say I didn't pen them verses
Desperately pulling moist skin around the gaping hole you left
Attempting to close unhealed wounds

Daddy I just want to know
Did you at least remember to pray for me?
Because I might gain a little piece of mind
If you considered me before our father
Resting assured that you cared a little

Daddy did you pray?
Did you?
Huh?
Did you hurt when you felt my absence?

I would love to say that I didn't want you to hurt
That I didn't want you to feel empty and guilty
Every time you hear my name
Getting whiplash from twisting your neck real fast
To see if I was somewhere in the room
Daddy did your absence from me pain you?

If it didn't that's fine too
Evidence that God blessed you mightily
By hardening your heart like Pharaoh's
Giving well placed callouses that you might not entertain
Guilt's strain
I'm sorry to say I didn't have the luxury of escaping that pain

But somehow I know that you didn't quite get away that clean
I know there had to be someone whispering 'bout me
Some person saying something
Not leisurely allowing you to deny your child

Daddy who advocated for me
Because there is no evidence that you did
Who championed for me
Besides my mother
Because she did the things that you should have done
And I ain't talkin' 'bout payin' bills and opening doors
But telling my siblings who I was

I remember those conversations they had
When she told each one of them that you were my dad
And they all looked at me for the first time
Recognizing that I was the girl who was always around
And the sister they never knew they had

Also being the youngest of them
My face was a reminder that at some point in time
You did they momma bad

Daddy who came up in your ear?

Was it any one of your peers who knew your cruel secret?
And had enough guts to speak the truth?
Was it God Himself who was angry enough to tongue lash you?
Daddy?
Huh?

Yeah
I'm still angry sometimes
You would think that after living this long
I would have let things go
But no

And believe me I tried
Tried to talk myself into believing that me being well
Was more important than you being there
I would go to God and try to pray away care

I could say that your absence made me better
And it taught me all of these things
And I am stronger
And I am a queen
And it would be true

But there is a truth
Deeper still that truthfully I am not stilled
And each time I find some peace of mind
And think I have forgiven you
Each time I stitch the wound
It's good and clean for a little while
Allowing me to forget and have a smile
Then puss begins to seep out
Proving this festering infection is at the very core of me
The antibiotic of ministry has not cured my scar tissue

No matter what I do
I can't get over you
And like the Apostle Paul had a thorn in his side
I guess I have mine too

And I have trust issues
Anger issues
And like other poets I got daddy issues
Maybe that's why I am a poet
Maybe that's why I am even any good
Which just pisses me off more
To know that I am who I am because of you
And I don't feel you deserve any credit

But maybe if I knew you prayed for me
I could get healing •

Trials of an Unclaimed Child: Unmentionables

Dear Unclaimed Child,

You are purposed.

Bastard child of the galaxy, you are still a star, a guiding light in a dark world.

The world will know your name.

Until then, shine.

Your light, beaming in the distance, whispers with a flicker ...

I exist.

Signed,

Your Unclaimed Sibling

Trials of an Unclaimed Child:
Deaths

I often mourn people
Based on the relationship we should have had
Stolen people
People I should have known from birth
Should have loved them
Gained wisdom from them
Should have had the opportunity to make choices
Like hating or adoring
Speaking or ignoring

I should have known their secrets
They should have been the source of my irritation
Or the river of peace soothing my hurts
We should have been as familiar as we are familial

But instead
I learn of their deaths via computer screens
Their pictures invade my news feed
Lingering in my thoughts
And lounging in my tear ducts

I remember the day I found out my grandmother died
I accidentally happened upon her face
On my morning scroll
Her image carried kind eyes
With a caption that said good bye ...

I wasn't afforded a hello

Broken Shards

Alice cracked the looking glass
The fractured sand refracted purple light
And it wasn't until she looked at her image through broken shards
That she realized she was royal

Restraint

This lump is a strain
Throat bulging, aching
Pressured larynx

Eye wells engorged
Threatening to spill
The evidence of torment

I feel like letting free
Yet I rebel against my own energy
And choose to be salty without the sea

These cheeks
Will not be the altar
Of wet prayers today

To Be: A Guide to Existing in Your Natural Skin

I. To Be Black
Must present black card
Must open carry
Steppin Fetchit
For those challenging your validity
Must have watched all the movies
And play a mean hand of spades
Just don't be a spade
Don't be a blithe
Don't embarrass us
Mustn't ember us
Become small so as to
Burn out and ash over
Disintegrate to dust
As they expect us to
We're only a fad you know
Wasn't s'posed to exist here long you know
They gon' be us one day you know

II. To Be Black and Woman
Must be forgiving
Must have had street lights on childhood
Unless you country
Must eat sunflower seeds and hot pickles
Make Kool-Aid sweet as your smile
Tangy as your attitude

Provide safety and solace
Bosom safe haven
Soft place for all men
No matter their natural born mothers
Respect, love, honor
Nurture the uncle that molested you
At family gatherings
Make his plate perfect

You know how he likes it
Sing and pray at his funeral
Unable to distinguish
Anguish from relief

Must be white wearing missionary
Never resting
Must care for your dozens
And throwaways of no use to society

Must mitigate epidemics
Repair and refurbish men
Caulk crack heads don't leak their secrets
Must be wet nurse providing milk
For kites to come down off sticks
And beds for distilleries to dry out in
Clothe them after their nakedness
Restore them to their right mind
Till next time
Must be there next time

III. To Be Black and Woman and Fat
Must be fierce
Must be outspoken
Must be bright
Must be brilliant
Must be bold

To be buxom
Must be beautiful
To excuse weight
Must be abnormally gorg'
Not bohemian
Or Badu
Must be willing to let that tummy show
Let wolves fetishize soft round
Prowl stretch marks
Get lost in thighs, folds, creases

Must have *donk*
Must be curvy
Must have big breasts
Bulging orbs of eye milk
Satiating them boys 'round midnight
Dark time feedings
Void morning time results

Can't be plain Jane
Can't be undesirable
Can't be soft spoken
Can't be just normal

Unless you mammy
Wear head wrap and apron
Can't eat
But CAN cook
It's permissible to cook
With all the good stuff
Fat back and "syrupy sweet"
Make pancakes
Feed yo' babies
They babies
Those babies
You hongry baby?
Must be open
Allow everyone in
Open home
Open mind
Open mouth
Open legs
Must be useful

Must be funny
Must laugh
Must be jolly
Must take the joke

Must operate under restriction
Can't eat meals in cars
Or on the go
Must wait until table
Like decent people do
As if they let you sit at the table
As if there was room at the table
As if they wanted to be seen with you
At their table
As if your weight didn't make them seem guilty
You didn't tell her she was fat?
Didn't you tell her to do something about that?
As if your weight was an indictment
As if your heavy weighed them down
Like the light of life is so minute
As to be overshadowed by rolls

Must be unseen
Must be unwanted
Must be lonely
Must be alone
Must pretend to be all things fat black women should be
Must be unknown

Love Over Weight

It's magic you know
Pretending not to be hungry
Makes necessity for nourishment disappear

It's magic you know
They stop staring if fat rolls
Are openly acknowledged
Justify eating and appetite
As if fat makes you less human
Oh I haven't eaten all day
Big as I am I shouldn't eat at all

It's magic you know
All the fat melts when you stop eating
Be void of ALL nutrition
Till ALL evidence of
Nutrition falls off

It's like water you know
I can survive on these gluten free
Calorie free
Sodium free
Dye free
Artificial flavoring free
Opinions
I just ain't got no discipline

They're like water you know
They look beneficial and necessary
Running right through me wreaking havoc
Flooding, tearing down everything I built up
Till self-esteem has nowhere to live and must be relocated
Here you have it!
Feel good about yourself!
At least you're not *this* fat

Your opinions are like water you know
Heavy and dense, torrential
Thinning out and eroding self-image
I will soon be emaciated
A skinny mess of insecurity inside all this meat on my bones

They're like water you know
Your thoughts
Your judgment
Your backseat physician diagnosis
Root Cause Analysis of Obesity
They come spilling out reckless
Yet you still ain't levied your mouth

Beginning Clowning — Lesson 1: Juggling

paint face with white face paint professional makeup
nose and cheeks red from crying but always wear lipstick
start slow — throw gas bill payment in the air

car note interest rate 28.5%
    plus $8.95 to pay by credit card
    plus $35 late fee
    plus pray for no traffic stops due to no insurance
    plus "well, can't you borrow it from a relative?"
    plus payment arrangement
    plus car repo (you can make arrangements & they'll still repo)
        plus $350 repo fee
        plus $150 per day lot fee
        plus $25 storage fee
        plus $150 fee for the fee people
        plus no pay for days off work
        plus $30 fare to get to work or lost job
        plus hungry mouths
plus payday loan #1
    plus 133% interest

catch light bill
throw water bill in the air — catch in 2 months
whoops! dropped the gas — shut off

    plus $200 deposit
    plus $75 reconnect fee
    plus the $37.50 late fee

whoops! fumbled rent

    plus $100 late fee and pissed landlord
    plus eviction notice
plus emergency assistance

My Mother the Cutter

She has an insatiable addiction
To self-mutilation
A few times she almost died
Inflicting pain
To rid pain
Bleeding her heart dry
Beating a tune of lonely and distrust
Compartmentalizing trauma
She'd open herself
Gape a hole
Filling the space in between
Slicing her slit
Open

These men cut deep

Trauma

I used to be eternity
Immeasurable
Shape-shift liquid spirit
Larger than containment
Spilling, splashing, squirting
I was the sea and
You enjoyed my ageless fluidity
Easy nature and beauty
Marveled at my unpredictability

And with one chilling experience
The once flowing temperament
Froze into an ice aged abyss
With no warmth to melt the damage
Freezer burned heart
Ruined
I found my waves polluted with trash heaps
Of trauma oil slicked sick
With no dawn to break the deterioration
Of my once pure state

But you
You that enjoyed the timelessness
Of my shores
Once before
Now became clocks
My timing to be commanded by
Tic
Toc

Stone faced walls
Staring me down
Quantifying the amount of
Time I could spend
Being emotional about this corruption

Believing that your limitations
Could transform my face
From marbled swirling color confusion
To concrete numbers
Something you could count on
Had always been able to rely upon
To remain the same
Smiling sun dial
That you never knew how to read
Tic
Toc

You wanted to moon my tides
Controlling how high I came in
Praying that I wouldn't swallow you whole

Added term limits to trauma
Measuring the amount of tears I could drop
Like you rule or something
Like you a ruler of something
You don't own

Trauma is not a calculable entity

This expanse does not run on your schedule
You clock
But I'm time
Electric, lunar, or solar
You have no power over me

I grieve as long as I need to grieve
I deny as long as I need to deny
My reality is mine
My hurt and healing are mine
After all that has already been taken
How dare you attempt to
Take the LAST thing that is mine

Desperately trying to levee my issues
But sincerely not giving a damn

And through my moment of vulnerability
You forgot my power and agility
I am not to be restrained

I flood and flood and flood
If you make me
If you do not allow this ice age
To follow the natural process to the next era
I will ruin you
Until there is no *me* left

Because in times of distress I have no limits
Knowing that someday you will need my oasis
I will be unforgivingly dry

I will desert
Willingly

As you couldn't even afford me
A moment of rain
Due to your own fear
Of me falling out of the sky
And crashing to the ground

Fool, don't you know certain parts of me
Have to go in to the ground for you to live?

And as you wither
Ashes to dust
Crumpled and dehydrated
Thirstily awaiting my presence

You will say
"She used to be water"

Nouveau Riche vs Melanin Rich

This beautiful brown, thick-lipped
Melanin-rich girl said she wanted
To be like those famous chicks

This gorgeous girl wanna be
On some matte-ish plump-ish shiny-ish
Kylie/Kim-ish type blackness

Inject and show off fake -*ish*
That manufactured beauty standard
Reborn on surgical steel

Fresh out of anesthesia
Swollen, discolored and tender type
Of *I woke up like dis cute*

Mismanaged a metaphor
Thought *Flawless* meant perfect rather than
Love me, take me as I am

So now she a wanna-be
Wannabe, wanna be something she's
Already gifted to be

American Logic

I
Protests where guns are present are not peaceful
Police carry guns
Police are present at protests
Protests are not peaceful

II
People are scared of the dark
My people are African
Africans have strong melanin
Melanin darkens the skin
One drop of blood makes you one of us
People are scared of us

III
Humans that kill each other are disposable
Blacks kill each other
Black lives are disposable

IV
Unless you completely submit, you are resisting arrest
A limp body cannot resist
Black bodies are strong
Black bodies lose physical power when limp
Limp bodies are normally dead
Lethal force is necessary for arrest

Super Unreal

many poems start with stargazing lyrics
rhythmical rhyming free verses
versus
tight structure
line for line imagination
and word bending

but this poem
this is a poem of my personal flight of fancy
a poem where reality knows its boundaries
and it dares not cause itself embarrassment
by attempting to box me in

reality knows better than to
try and shut me down in this poem
and maybe to someone this poem means nothing
but has been in me since i was a child
tying the towel around my neck
pretending to be a caped crusader
running through the cracked concrete on hot sweaty days
jumping off the jungle gym
scraping my knees
jumping to my feet crying
running home bleeding
this poem is blood sweat and tears
so i could care less if others identify
THIS POEM IS FOR ME
this poem is about what my mom and my **GOD** made me to be
i'm a freakin
super cool
super awesome
karate chop
ralph macchio high jump kick
scientific
SUPER HERO

'cause my momma
is a freakin'
kristi love
action jackson
afro
black power
with the fist at the end
of the pick
x-men
antidisestablishmentarianist
SUPER HERO

at the sound of a crying child
she could leap a playground slide in a single bound

with her super strength
she could braid your eyebrow
connect it to your hairline
back around to your nose hairs
whoop your behind
and watch *young and the restless*
all at the same time

with her power of mental persuasion
she make me believe we were **RICH**
in fact this power of mental persuasion was so strong
that sometimes even **SHE** forgot we were broke

no really
we wore the finest linens
because my momma could sew
had a mind to revitalize
thrift store skirts, shirts and ties
into the latest fashions

we ate at the best gourmet restaurants
because she could cook

we indulged in the most elite entertainment
because for hours I had to dance
in tap shoes on that kitchen floor
to that **MICHAEL JACKSON** *BAD* cd
kick ball change - kick ball change - kick ball change

had fine china dollar store plastic dishes
to play kitchen with
second-hand roller skates
my julie talking doll
and my teddy ruxpin
strawberry shortcake room décor
pink carpet on the floor

and I was **BOSS** with my high water jeans
jheri curl and wooden beads
snaggletoothed
fly custom made easter fit
dig it
i used to travel to different worlds
reading rainbow style
via book passage
and playground

didn't have video games
but we did have scrabble
parcheesi, dominoes, solitaire and spades
even had a commodore 24 vic 20
with whack-a-mole and cassette tape games

we had nearly nothing
and almost everything
because my momma had super powers

we had nearly nothing
and almost everything
because my momma had super powers

she could make things appear without money
get toilet paper and food with no ends
because she always helped others
so she had resources and friends

no five-finger discount
because on the law she did not bend
she always kept it honest
never renege on a promise

but the one thing her super powers could not do
was hide the kryptonite truth
and even though she didn't want to cry in front of me
i knew her vulnerabilities
even though she didn't disclose all of her past and memories
i knew she had dreams unachieved

so i vowed that when i grew up
i was going to be just like my mom
a super hero
i will tie on my bathroom towel
like a caped crusader
reaching in with my super intuitive x-ray spirit vision
and correct her self-esteem
that she may regard herself as a **QUEEN**
quit settling for the court jester
and hold out for the **KING**

i will use my invisible mental probe
to change her mind
so she won't fault herself
for problems of mine
momma
i will use my super speed
fast enough to generate heat
gather the sand granules of
your broken heart
and force them together till they are complete

and with my super power of healing
i would revive
GOD'S original design
secure your mind
and make you understand
that it is okay
to trust
and it's all right
if a man takes the lead
you ain't gotta be independent all the time

i will take my trust restoration snipe rocket
and demolish the childhood demons
that caused you to become a super hero
in law enforcement blue
the same demons that had you running home from school

and no one ever knew the cause for this desire
to save damsels and put out fires

and now that i have super powers
there are some things that i would not do
i wouldn't hurry up and buy that new 'lac
i would leave you with your ford ltd and pontiac
i would leave me with my
consignment store clothes
and dollar store dishes
because lack is where inspiration is cultivated
and i made all my best wishes

and this wish has been in me since i was a child
you were there
when we had nothing
and i played using my imagination
tying the towel around my neck
pretending to be a caped crusader
running through the cracked concrete on hot sweaty days
jumping off the jungle gym

scraping my knees
jumping to my feet crying
running home bleeding
this poem is blood sweat and tears
when you wiped the tears mixed with sweat from my face
and bandaged my bloody wounds
so i could care less if anyone else anywhere identifies
THIS POEM
openly thanks **GOD** for a parent
who realized that it wasn't always about all you could give
but that it was about all that we had
and we had so much more than what could be held in hands
THIS POEM IS FOR YOU
because i as a grown woman believe in super heroes
my **SUPER HERO** just happens to be **YOU**

Super Unreal II

I thought I wanted to be a super hero.
Then, I discovered its harsh reality:

That once you become super,
There is no longer an option for human;
That in most episodes,
You aren't afforded a sidekick;
That carrying all this womb and man
Ain't the same as having super strength;
That flying into action
Doesn't come with invisible planes;
That the lasso of truth
often came with a noose;
That the cape had bad wind resistance,
So when the spirit hits we cry rivers,
Irrigating nothing but flooding with regret;
That all mountains aren't composed of rock,
So moving them requires more than hands.

Oh my God!
After I found out what *super*
Combined with *hero* really means
I ain't really wanna be no super hero

I only wanted to
Tie the bathroom towel around my neck
Pretending to be a caped crusader
Running through the cracked concrete
On hot sweaty days
And jump off the jungle gym

And now, for some reason when I jump
Instead of imagining myself flying
Soaring through the sky …
I end up grounded.

Faux Repair

Dear Activist,
Band-aids ain't neva been glue, but it'll do.

Warmest regards
Busted, Spilled, and Spent

P.S. Fake it till you make it, leaks and all.

####

Dear Busted,
No wonder we're still falling apart.

With love,
Activist

P.S. Old wine. New skin.

Delusional Activism:
Instructions

Instructions for Delusional Activism

To turn ashes to *ase*:
Wear Dashikis at the vigil.

Stand at the spot of blood spatter.
Take somber faced pictures.

Pose.
Post.

Rinse.
Repeat.

Delusional Activism:
Expectations

I am a woman who regularly attempts, while dining, to cut food with the wrong side of the knife but who never does this when cooking. I suppose if a butter knife can cut butter, then it should be able to successfully shred through whatever tender concoction I have prepared, no matter what side I use.

I have the same expectation for food I order at dining establishments. Certainly, if I am paying for YOU to make it, then it better well surpass, or at least be on par with, my skill.

I am often disappointed. Pissed even.

I have cut an entire Eggs Benedict, with a thick slice of ham, using the backside of a butter knife! You mean to tell me that I cannot do the same with this supposedly "tender" chicken breast FILLET! *(Not even a full half but FILLETED!)*

> *NAH SON!*
> *Y'all foul for this yo!*

I suppose I have high expectations, which is not due to my own attempts at deprogramming myself of such foolishness. I have told myself to suspend my beliefs so many times that I think I see day dreams *floating* over my head in mid-air, taking on the shapes of the clouds. I have preached the gospel of low expectations more times than I can count. Yet here I am, still expecting stuff and whatnot.

Foolishness!

I mean, I have high expectations of myself. At least I can control those. I suppose others just do not live by the same set of rules.

For example, a woman becomes pregnant. She carries the baby to term while providing proper nutrition, medical care, and vitamins. She reads to the baby in the womb. She counts rote numbers and sings to the child, prays over the child, and maintains a healthy relationship with the father of the child. The child is born and shows somewhat normal development for the first year of life. Then, she realizes her worst fears: a malady presented itself over a period of time. Her child was developmentally delayed!

She is scared and restless. She takes the baby to as many doctors as she can, including therapists. She tries and tries, knowing that this ailment is something that her child will have to live with for the rest of his/her life.

Here is how I feel about *The Movement* of Black Americans. And I know I am not supposed to have all these expectations. Heck, I am not even the mother who carried and nurtured that baby! But I am a black woman—a mother—and my womb aches when I look at our people.

My heart falls into a puddle of disenchantment, flailing and splashing, yet eventually succumbing to disappointment and drowning. The love for my people is well and alive, but the will to be involved in any of these *movements* is a dead thing that I carry in my chest.

I am tired.

I am tired of our own cries: "What about black on black crime?" It's as if we cannot focus on ALL of our tragedies at one time. It's as if there are not enough of us to do multiple things simultaneously. It's as if we are good for only one thing at a time, else we overload the capacity of a WHOLE PEOPLE GROUP.

Are we not intersectional? Are we not those who encompass much?

I promise that if the sentence starts with, "Until we stop," then it will end with something that will NOT stop our problems. It is not logical.

For example, children do not rape one another in high numbers. Why are there still pedophiles? Or women aren't raping one another in high numbers. Why are there still rapists?

The fact that a certain segment of people is not doing something to themselves does not prevent people from outside of that group from doing something to them. It just doesn't.

Don't tell me, "Until we stop." Until we stop what? Until we stop killing each other, people outside of our people group will not respect our humanity?

The humanity of other people groups is respected, yet it doesn't stop people outside of their group from killing them. You heard NUTHIN' about "white on white crime" after Columbine (or any of the other tragic school shootings in white neighborhoods). It's not even a *thing* people say. You heard NUTHIN' about "white on white crime" when the conversation is about serial killers or Brock Turner. NO. That narrative is controlled down to the naming of names. It was this person. He was this tall, this old, had this color eyes, did this thing. Here are his mother, father, family history. In the "white crime" narrative, the criminals are first humans who somehow become "monsters."

Even in the scenario where they do not know who did the crime, if the crime happened in the white community to a white person, then the narrative is displayed in a different way. There is still one person who is a monster: one kidnapper, one rapist, one murderer. That community separates themselves from this monster. Law enforcement sings the praises of the innocent and makes direct threats against the perpetrator. They make a stand. They say, "We are going to find this monster, so help us God." And everyone watching knows that they mean business. It is not a façade. They certainly mean business. After all, they live in the same neighborhood. You wouldn't want a monster on the loose in your neighborhood. Would you?

Then you've got *us*. Robbie kills Tarick because Tarick broke into

Robbie's home. Why do we know who Tarick is? We only know who Tarick is because Tarick is dead. And then, we throw the "black on black crime" flag on the play. In the media, an activist speaks about black on black crime, and the murmuring about Robbie begins. "What did he have in that house?"

When Cody kills Tyler for breaking in his home in a white When Cody kills Tyler for breaking into his home in a white neighborhood, it may not make the news. If it does, then there is no murmuring about Cody and what's in his home. He is just a white man, protecting his home, his family, and his valuables. He is an American with 2nd Amendment rights. He did what any American *should* do. Robbie, however, is perceived as somehow less than American: not un-American, just less. Even his possessing a firearm comes into question.

Black on black crime isn't even a *thing*. No, it is not! Don't argue this with me. I will simply say this: Is it really "black on black crime" if we are not calling out other races for their crimes against one another? Or is it just a crime of proximity and opportunity? My vote is for the latter. Is "Latin on Latin crime" a *thing*? Is "white on white," or "Asian on Asian," or "Greek on Greek" crime a *thing*? Surely, this naming convention isn't purely focused on numbers and crime rates. Hmmm ... interesting.

Everyone knows you can take advantage of black folk and no one will *cape* for us. The world knows we have no heroes. Yes the world knows, including black criminals.

When black folk used to say "black on black crime," it was a murmur, an internal conversation. It was the type of thing only said among *family*. Now, after we throw the "black on black crime" label on an incident, we proudly stand on the news, blogs, and social media shouting "BLACK ON BLACK CRIME" to the mountain tops while crying a river of Negro tears. The black community's actions are reactionary and caused by fear.

Crime is never just crime with us. Crime is its own monster. It has no faces, no names. It is just black. It is all of us and any of us. Our whole race is dehumanized. On the news, there are no police proclaiming threats upon this human monster. I suppose police are afraid of boogeymen, too.

We look at each other with unreasonable suspicion. Perpetrators are never caught; they get away with it. No one speaks their names; they are urban legends. Stories of them are whispered in the streets. No one says their names aloud for fear of badge wearers infiltrating our hoods ... or worse, the fear that the monster will come after them.

We can say that the names are not said to protect the community, the innocent, or whomever. But the truth of the matter is this: when the business of eradicating crime is in the hands of the white community, they control how much information is published through the media. If the they do not want to release information about little Katy getting raped, then it will not happen.

The "black on black crime" narrative tells the whole world that we don't have our selves together, that we are not in order. It opens the door to insult and criticism, enabling the use of "until" statements by outsiders: *Until ya'll stop killing ya'll selves, how can you expect us to stop killing you?!*

We have helped to craft this narrative.

We have helped to craft this narrative. And because we buy into this thought process, we agree with their "until" statements and say, "They're right. How can we expect them to respect our humanity until we respect it ourselves?" We create marches, rallies, and vigils with no action attached. They are the same as showing up to church every Sunday while leading a Godless life.

It seems our progress as a people is a bit developmentally delayed and leaning towards permanent disability.

I am appalled. I am tired. But I had these expectations.

The civil rights era was romanticized through Dr. King and "bad boy" fetishized through Malcolm X. It was conscious through Marcus Garvey yet studious through W.E.B. Du Bois. It was powerful through Angela Davis yet sexy through Josephine Baker. It made me want to be a non-violent, by any means necessary. It made me an enterprising, sexy member of the talented tenth. I wanted to be BLACK. In the words of Dr. Yaba Blay, I wanted to be "a professional black girl." I wanted to be the kind of black girl who could always SHUT IT DOWN with dancing, food, poetry, arithmetic, hair, history, and professionalism. ALL THAT.

I wanted to be a part of the people that were all of these things. The fighters! The activists! The educators! The community builders! The front line standers! They all were the healers, and I wanted to be a healer. I had passion, yo!

Then, I grew up and realized that all that passion I had (and honestly still have) should not have to exist. I look at my children and see what our predecessors were fighting for. I look at the condition of the world and see that my children—both familial and the ones that I have had the pleasure of mentoring—may also become activists.

I don't think that Malcolm, Martin, Newton, Bethune, Angela Davis, Sojourner Truth, or any of the like wanted the next generations, and the next, and the next to have to fight the way we do. I don't think that they purposefully said, "My children and my children's children will be activists." Revolutionaries and leaders, maybe. There will always be a need for a revolutionary mind set, one that is proactive and innovative. There will always be a need for good leadership. There should not be a need for an activist.

Our great leaders expected to work themselves out of a job. They expected that through education, however it was achieved (speeches, non-violent resistance, protesting, screaming, being the best of the best, etc.), that we would be seen as human. They experienced victories and won battles. They watched as people, both black and white, were killed on the front lines of this fight.

They saw blood coming from two different humans mix on the ground. They saw both black and white bleed together, and the naked eye couldn't tell what blood belonged to whom.

Now, I find myself looking at my children, wondering what battles they will have to fight and wondering if my children's children will still be fighting the same battles on the same two battlefields: (a) the battlefield of their own community and its mindset, and (b) the battlefield of the rest of the world.

I pray not. I expect so much more for them. But if I cannot successfully cut a supposedly tender chicken breast fillet with the back of a butter knife, then I cannot expect their soft innocence to cut through the tribulations of this world and survive it. I had better make sure that both sides of my children are sharp. They can't be just butter knives; they also must be swords.

It is a shame that I still have to teach my children that they must be ten times better than everyone else, that they must run faster and fight harder, that they must be sharp and pointed and metal and resilient, that they must be iron and sharpen each other, that they must be hard and strong and unbreakable and unable to be sliced, and that they must be this and that in order to excel while black.

I expected my work, the work of my contemporaries, and the work of those that came before me to protect my children's tender loving, innocence, but my expectations are way too high. Your expectations probably are too.

So, let my words be a lesson to you. I am a preacher of the Gospel of Low Expectations, and I encourage you to monitor and manage your expectations. Be patient. Continue the work. Continue the fight. Continue to educate and speak. Push on. We aren't there yet, and we shouldn't be expected to be.

Delusional Activism:
Black on Black Crime

Black on black crime
Is an urban legend
Is creative and crafted
Media propaganda
Promoted, problematic, and paid for
Is fetishized
Is an oasis of scary prime time sensationalism
For a hallucinogenic people
Is a scripted trope
Is glorified violence
Is not all inclusive
They never call suicide
Black on black crime
Never call the murder of a black cop by a black person
Black on black crime
Guess he's blue
Guess his badge makes him not black
Makes him not matter
They never call domestic violence
Black on black crime
Never call rape or molestation
Black on black crime
Guess we're too sexual
Even when we're not
Even when we don't want it
Even when we say no
Black on black crime
Is blood soaked ground imagery
Is *brothas* need to keep themselves 'cause ain't no keepers
Is expecting black women to keep keeping *brothas*, secrets & kids
Is an open door to faux-tepisms
Is conscious as of yesterday
Is "It's all these damn single mothers" reasoning
Is pretending Eve ain't have a husband

Ain't have no father in the home
Is a backwards excuse for Cain
Is an Ablest mentality
'Cause niggas been doin' this since the beginning of time
'Cause niggas gon' be niggas
This all niggas seen and all niggas do
Is "It ain't no dumpin' all wild
I focus in on a target
He *tha* tallest in *tha* crowd"
Is Guick Draw McGraw in blackface
But isn't celebrated like cowboys and Indians
Is hypermasculine and aggressive
Is hopless, helpless
Is the Ursula of Disney rather than Hans Christian Andersen
Is overly dramatized and malevolent
Is drag queen caricature, mammy or whore
Is character creation and assassination at the same white hands
Is whacked and drugged out
Animalistic and wild
Is sexy monsters having a ball all while loosing Isaiah
Is awarded and critically acclaimed
Is watching the nightly news as if it's National Geographic
Is the biased study of the environment but not its causes
Is a theory
A myth
A racist narrative
Because the black boy who killed the other black boy
Didn't do so because he was black
Or because he saw his reflection
Didn't rob her because of her skin
Didn't attack them for melanin
But because of lack
Or greed
Or jealousy
Infidelity
Deception
Mental distress
Sin

Or any of the other human conditions
Other races have
Black on black crime
Is condemnation
Damnation
Victimization
And vilification done by 4 words
Is people perishing from lack of this knowledge
While looking for a solution to this
Black on black crime
Construct
It is not law
Not science
Not our culture
Not a *thing*
Not who we are
Not real
We are not animals
It is not instinct
The **BLACK ON BLACK CRIME** label is bondage
Is bondage
Is bondage
And at the quake of this realization
My dungeon shook
And my chains finally fell off

Delusional Activism:
A Friendly Reparations Request

Because we know you are good people

When you give us our reparations can you—
Give us more than 40 acres and one unbreedable animal?
Give us the men who work the land?
Give back the time spent locked away from family and children?
Resurrect the lives stolen?

Will you replace the china?
The dining room table?
The old porcelain dolls?
The art and artifacts?

Will you reconstitute our dried lineages?

They are the ones from when we had to flee
With just the clothes on our backs.

We wrestled water bodies and pretzeled our lungs
As the current decapitated tribal wisdom.

It ripped the family tree from limb to limb
Carrying the knowledge of our ancestors downstream.

Our lost heritage washed up on the shores.
Can you send out search parties, rescue and restore?

Will you give us our hip-hop back?
Will you give the credits due?
Can we at least own that?

Our rhythms (the natural *boom de boom bap*)
In our backs that you replaced with crack crack crack.

Crack the whip
Crack the dome
Crack rocks
Made crack spots
Stepped on crack
Broke many mothers' backs
Had them raising their children's children.

Will you un-mother our grandmothers?
Can they just be grand?
Can they rest as a place of reverence?
A protected species instead of a necessary extinction?

Will you return our women?
Un-rape, un-maim, and un-slain our women?
Restore virtue and respect?

If you could please
Also replace the Hottentot
With your body parts.
She been working far too long.

And after we receive all these things,
Can you resist the urge to torch our success?
Can you not burn us down like black wall street?
Our increase rubbled at our feet.

If you could please
Repay
Refund
Recompense
Reimburse
Remunerate
(I dare not say reparate).

Then, after that, just leave us be.
It would put an end to unrest spanning centuries.

Delusional Activism:
Stay Woke

Word to the wise.

Sleep.

Please sleep.

Please get some rest.

Sleep detoxifies and heals the body and the mind, alleviates stress, and according to studies, the human body grows more while sleeping than awake.

Sleeping for at least 1/3 of the day is good.

SLEEP is GOOD.

When we are woke, we choose the things that we are *woke* to just as much as we choose the things that we are *sleep* to.

Impure thoughts and selfish gain are often cleansed when a person is not involved where they should not be. Everyone should not *cape* for your cause. It doesn't meant that said *non-capeing* persons are *sleep*; it simply means that they are staying in their own lanes: A.K.A **SUPER WOKE**.

People that stay in their own lanes find rest.
Find your lane.

Stay in your lane.
Rest there.

Black women that are *sleep*, or "airheads," are just as valuable as those that are so-called *conscious*. They may be *sleep* to marching in the streets but are *woke* to their families. They may be *sleep* to current events but are *woke* to nourishing and loving. They may be *sleep* to protesting but are *woke* to praying for you at 3:00 am during your peaceful slumber. There are some that are *woke* to none of this and simply awaiting direction and a path. Be patient.

WE ARE ALL VALUABLE.
WE ALL STILL LOVE.
WE ALL HEAL.
WE ALL HAVE TRUTH.

I can attest to the fact that many people have attempted to pull me in directions that were not meant for me, tried to attack the heart that I wore on my sleeve by pulling me by its string. I have come to discover that though they rang the alarm, that alarm was not for me. It may have been for them (or someone else in the house), but that wakeup call was not for me. Do I care? Of course! Does it matter? Sure! Can I be all things to all people and all causes? Certainly not! I do not operate under that expectation.

Don't allow people to pull you in to seemingly worthy causes with emphatic emotional reasoning. Many movements are formed around mis-information and bias. So while you think you are being *woke*, you are *sleep* walking.

Honestly, many that claim *consciousness* are just regular folks with too much information in their heads. These same people will never use a fraction of that information, except to tear others down, in which case amounts to the importance of an answer in a game of *Jeopardy!*

Please stop pitting us against one another. Love the person **YOU** believe is *sleep* just as much as the person that is **YOU** believe is *woke*.

#myRESTgamestrong
#chillyo
#MLKhadaDREAM
#HemusthavebeenSLEEP

Gold Repair

Dear Life,
You tried it.

Signed,
Broken (but not destroyed)

The Potter

I
Broken pottery

HE
Artisan Creator
Kept every piece
Tossing away nothing
Recognizing value
Even in brokenness

Cracks became tools
To tell the story
The rock-bottom gory
The splintering crash
Hearts' shattered pieces
Dashed across the land

The devastating drop
From a loved one's hands
From a heart that
Should have cupped and held close
Should have been precious
Should have remained whole
Undamaged

HIS hand steady
Master repair
Goldsmith
Piecing together
Making cracks solid
Water proof
Impenetrable
Protected
Loved again
Useful again
Clean and beautiful

This time with
Precious elements
Metals
Jewels
Redesigned
More valuable than before
More valued than before
Renewed
Refreshed
Remastered

Squiggly lines
Hard zig zags
Meandering curves
Sealed with gold
Testifying of glory
And fulfilled promise
HIS power of creation
And recreation
Illuminated!
Through my victory

The Restorer

He's not perfect or ideal
He's unreal
An oxymoron

He's wonderful
Wonder and wonderment
Concrete hard flexibility
He moves for me

He is comfort and extravagance
Fluffy featherbed and Egyptian cotton
Prime rib and potatoes, hot sauce and neck bones
Utilitarian with frills

He's a lil' bit extra
Flashing anger and blue calm
Nerve irksome confusing simplicity
Holy hellion and healing balm

He's 85% dark chocolate
Strong taste and enough sweet
He's a strange football ritual
That tickles my fancy

He's all I never had
And more than what I signed up for
Proof God is still working
Proof God restores

He's all things
All mine
All I dreamed
And never thought to ask for

He sees my faults
And thinks perfection of me
Full of spewing lecture and freely forgiving
He is the most human and imperfect being
But he still manages to love me Godly
And that's all I need

Sanctuary

In the glimpse of a day dream
For a second
I can return home
Then lose home again

Weary spirit
And worn sole
Souls nomadically holy
Searching for the holy of holies

Safety
Solace
Solitude
So tired of

Tired

Being
Human
Living less than
A human

Being

The facade of
Completeness
Hides the reality
Of a complete mess

Chosen child of the King
Reduced to rat races
Chasing nonexistent
Finish lines

But here

The altar of your presence
I rest peacefully in your sacred space
Release regrets
And effortlessly love

Immune from arrest of the unwelcome
Arrested in the caress of comfort
Leaving the whole world behind
Just for this moment

Only to lose it at the button of a colored collar
Tic toc of a clock
Clock into the work of the world
With too few prayers

Ill-equipped to handle Pan and his nature
I pan handle in the wild
From corners to franchise
Chasing the same dime

I find the image of my stolen moment
And transform the chaos of my mind
To relive the sanctuary
Surviving only on this borrowed time

Transcend

I am the breath of fresh air
My own lungs have longed for

Light and fluffy
Airy as a Caribbean breeze off the water tingling my skin

Luminous and glowing
Floating and free

Spirit challenging flesh boundaries
Beaming rays of radiance

Darkness attempted
To box a divinity it couldn't comprehend
Shining through its fractured cracks
Beauty through containment

I am anywhere and everywhere I want to be
I am who I want to be
I am what I want to be
I am more than a conqueror

And there is nothing out of my reach

I eclipse the sad tragedy and the statistic
My cloud looms over pain and I reign
Royal throne
I crown
Rebirth

New beginnings
I genesis
I bang big galaxy
I'm more important than the star I create

My meteors have impact and hit hard
I impress
Hearts and minds
Leaving my mark on souls
I live on

I am the wind
A change agent
Tornado whipping landscapes
And in the same breath
Softly caressing cheeks

Light
Me

I am flames that both rubble and refine

I can do all things through omnipresent brilliance
Shimmering tenacity inside of me

I am enough
And so much more

I am the breath of fresh air my own lungs have longed for

I transcend

Own It: A Discourse on Sex/Sensuality

1. *Own it.* You are not your virginity or lack thereof. You are a human, not to be identified by what you have or have not done. Don't be intimidated by those who seek to take part in it; you owe it to no one.

2. *Own it*. She is beautiful. Gaze at her, smile, and be friendly. Women are beautiful. Take it all in. Loving the beauty of a woman doesn't change your sexuality; it doesn't make you confused. It only makes you human with an honest set of eyes.

3. *Own it.* She is beautiful and so are you. Acknowledge her, love her, befriend her, build a sisterhood. There is no competition between sisters.

4. *Own it.* Investigate. Ask Questions. Ask yourself. Ask him. Do you feel protected? Will he harm you? Has he promised to do life with you? Don't give valuables in the hope of receiving a forever. You are a jewel. You are the treasure, not the addition to his collection.

5. *Own it.* Laugh. Do you laugh together or is he too busy trying to be funny? Do you laugh full belly laughs holding yourselves together? Do you laugh until tears fall, slobber forms, and your stomach aches? Do you laugh while looking at each other? Laughter is a different level of intimacy most will never know. Laughter can heal. Laughter is the best medicine. Laughter has the power to reach to the soul, restore, and make joy out of pain.

6. *Own it.* Forgive. Forgive its tingle, its moisture, its excitement. *That* is all a part of who she is. Forgive, when it did all of this and you were terrified in your heart. Forgive, when it did all of this and you were attacked. Forgive, when it did all of this and you were raped. Forgive, when it still does this as an after-effect of abuse (and it feels inappropriate). Forgive, when it wasn't able to clamp down hard, shut tight, and not let the intruder in. Forgive yourself

for not being able to protect her. Forgive before doubting your self-worth. Forgive, so that you can move on to healthier pastures.

7. _Own it._ You are not what happened to you. You are who God says you are, no less.

8. _Own it._ Know it. Name it. Give it a name. No matter if you never mention it to another living soul, you should be on a first name basis. Smell it. Know its nuances, its changes. Know the feel of it. For health, maturity, and pleasure, it is a requirement.

9. _Own it._ Know it. Savor it. Enjoy it. Explore it, safely. Are you comfortable enough to learn yourself with him? Learn how to get on and get off and be honest enough to tell him when you didn't. Be free. Can you be free with him? Allow your mind to go, breasts to bounce, sweat to drop, mouth to open, and sounds to come out. Pay no mind to the fat roll or the sound it makes. Own this moment. Revel in the clapping and the squishing. Don't be embarrassed at the wetness. Know that you are second to none. At least one time in life, call your own name. Then, smile and giggle a little, letting the fire light in your eyes. Laugh hard at that. Yes, he will be confused. Then, he will laugh with you. Be bold, brazen. It's not taboo; it's just you. It's good to be good at what you do. And if you find yourself in a situation where you feel the need to lie and say, "I have never done this before," he may not be the one for you. Run. And run fast before giving yourself, because this will not last.

10. _Own it._ Know it. Save it. If you cannot do any of this, you are not ready. You do not fully own your sexuality; so, you must keep predators at bay. They can smell un-surety and will surely eat you alive, leaving you broken. All the king's horses and all the king's men can't put it back together again. So, no sitting on the wall. No playing on the fence. No teeter tottering between he loves me, he loves me not, only to decide if you will bless him. No. The word is _KNOW._ Know that you are a blessing. Know it with no apologies. And if you know that you don't know, lock it away, because it is yours. And they must respect what you say.

Own It II

Happiness
Buzzy, Bright
Intoxicates, Exhilarates, Raptures
But doesn't stay unless it's claimed
On Purpose

If ...

If you have lost faith
If you are tired
If you are sooo done with this
If you question your beliefs
If you are unsure

If ...

Be healed today
Renewed
Whole
Smile
Laugh
Be restored

Today is your day

Evidenced by lungs that swell
And deflate
And swell again

Evidenced by the tears
And sorrow
And pain you have experienced that led you here

Evidenced by the hope that lingers in you
Know it HAS to get better (because it cant get any worse)
Know you are blessed, loved
Know there is one sent with a specific assignment
To pray for you
To hold you dear

If nothing else
Rejoice and be glad in this
•

Ellipses

Love poems are never truly written
They are born
You are a love poem

You, who were an unplanned pregnancy
Almost aborted
Adopted
Abandoned

You, whose mother made you feel hated
As if she regretted your birth
Whose family made you feel you weren't good enough

You, the one who the kids picked on in school
The one who is too fat
Too skinny
Too dark
Too light
Too quiet
You, who feels alone at night and cries

You are a song
A lullaby
An epic piece of literature with free will
Jumping line to line
Written across history

You are the verb and the noun transcending parts of speech
Both proper and improper
The majority of existing words ain't nuthin' without
U is a vowel that makes language beautiful

Yet you try to cut your narrative short
Attempt to rewrite yourself into an elegy
Snort your lines

Rearrange your free verse with self-hatred and pity
Binge drink into a tragedy
Making your pain a comedy of errors

You became your own abusive relationship
And made self-loathing a run-on sentence

You wrote hate speech across your arms and in your veins
Swallowed pill-shaped lies

Removed quotation marks from others beliefs
While striving to adopt them as your own
Because for sooo long you had nothing to identify with

You've replaced commas with periods out of fear
Replaced passages of hurt with dashes to move past them faster
Then added multiple exclamation points to pretend you've healed

You've looked for other mixed up poems to enjamb with
Only to find that you couldn't complete each other's stanzas

You've buried yourself in studies
To learn and manipulate your structure

You've tried to fit your novel into sonnets and haikus
Suffocating your form

But love was not meant to be that short

Love,
You ARE a love poem

A beautiful narrative of sacred and desecrated hills and valleys
Extreme joy and deep depression

You are an overcomer to be read aloud
You were meant to be heard

We are sonic
We are noise

We
Yes
Even me
Overweight me
Carmel
Sensitive skinned me
Imperfect
Abused
Lied on
Cheated on
Scarred and scared me

Who was born out of adultery
To a deacon who still doesn't claim me

I vow to be the loudest secret anyone has ever seen
My voice will ring from the asphalt to the mountain tops
Our spirits will raise souls from tombs
We will build a new world
A new world where all poems can be heard

We are a love poem
And though they tried to crumble our wide rule into a small ball
Tried to forget us all
We could never be thrown away
We are a love poem

The *author* is not yet finished ...

Sheri Purpose Hall is an author, minister, mentor, and counselor throughout the Kansas City metro area. She shares her time and energy with people of all ages, teaching courses in communications, writing to heal, poetry, and spoken word.

www.spokenpurpose.com